You are to prepare for the
invasion of Europe, for
unless we can go and land
and fight Hitler and beat
his forces on land, we
shall never win this war.
-- Winston Churchill
October 1941

In the last great invasion...

Of the last great war...

The greatest danger for eight men...

...was saving one.

saving private ryan

The Men. The Mission. The Movie.

A Film by Steven Spielberg

Photographs by David James

B XTREE

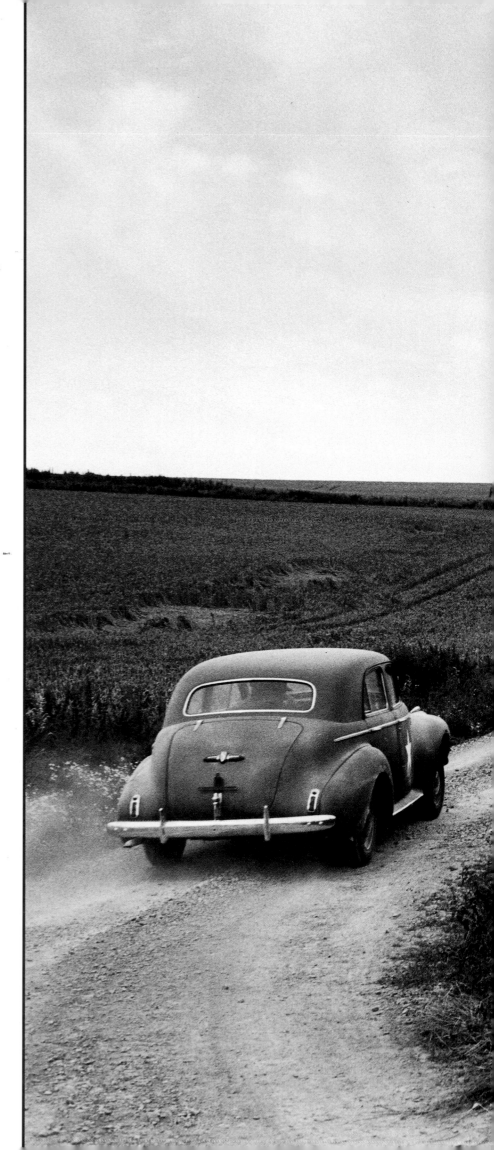

First published 1998 by Newmarket Press, New York

First published in Great Britain 1998 by Boxtree
an imprint of Macmillan Publishers Ltd
25 Eccleston Place London SW1W 9NF
and Basingstoke

Associated companies throughout the world

ISBN 07522 1348 2

9 8 7 6 5 4 3 2 1

A CIP catalogue record for this book is available from
the British Library.

Printed by The Bath Press, Bath

Page 17 Text used with permission from *The 101st Airborne at Normandy*
by Mark Bando and published by MBI Publishing, Osceola, Wisconsin.

Pages 15, 19, 21, 22 Text reprinted with the permission of Simon &
Schuster, Inc. from *D-Day: June 6, 1944, The Climactic Battle of World
War II* by Stephen E. Ambrose. New York: Simon & Schuster, 1994.
Copyright © 1994 by Ambrose-Tubbs, Inc. All Rights Reserved.

Pages 28, 33, 36 Text reprinted with the permission of Simon &
Schuster, Inc. from *Citizen Soldiers: The U.S. Army from the Normandy
Beaches to the Bulge to the Surrender of Germany June 7, 1944– May 7,
1945* by Stephen E. Ambrose. New York: Simon & Schuster, 1997.
Copyright © 1997 by Ambrose-Tubbs Inc. All Rights Reserved.

Pages 24-5, 29, 31 *Voices of D-Day: The Story of the Allied Invasion
Told by Those Who Were There.* Edited by Ronald J. Drez. Baton Rouge:
Louisiana State University Press, 1994. Copyright © 1994 by The
Eisenhower Center for Leadership Studies. All Rights Reserved.

Edited by Linda Sunshine.

Design by Timothy Shaner, Night & Day Design.

DreamWorks Project Executive: Jerry Schmitz
DreamWorks Photo Editor: Boyd Peterson
DreamWorks Art Director: Randy Nellis

INTRODUCTION

Set during and immediately following the invasion of Normandy, *Saving Private Ryan* tells the story of a squad of American soldiers on a dangerous mission to find Private James Ryan whose three brothers have been killed in combat. On direct orders from Washington, Captain John Miller leads his men deep behind enemy lines. As the squad pushes on, the men find themselves asking: Why is one man worth risking the lives of eight?

Amid the chaos and terror of those days in early June 1944, this remarkable story searches to find decency in the sheer madness of war.

While preparing to film *Saving Private Ryan*, hundreds of people spent countless hours researching and re-creating the battles, the landscape, and the destruction of France during those days. One thousand soldiers were employed in filming the landing on Omaha Beach. Original landing boats, guns, and gear were restored to working order. While shooting the battle scenes in strict chronological order, tens of thousands of rounds of ammunition were fired. Every effort was made to capture the harsh reality of war as authentically as possible.

World War II was perhaps the pivotal event of the twentieth century and a defining moment for America and the world. It shifted the borders of the globe, forever changed those who survived it, and shaped the past five decades.

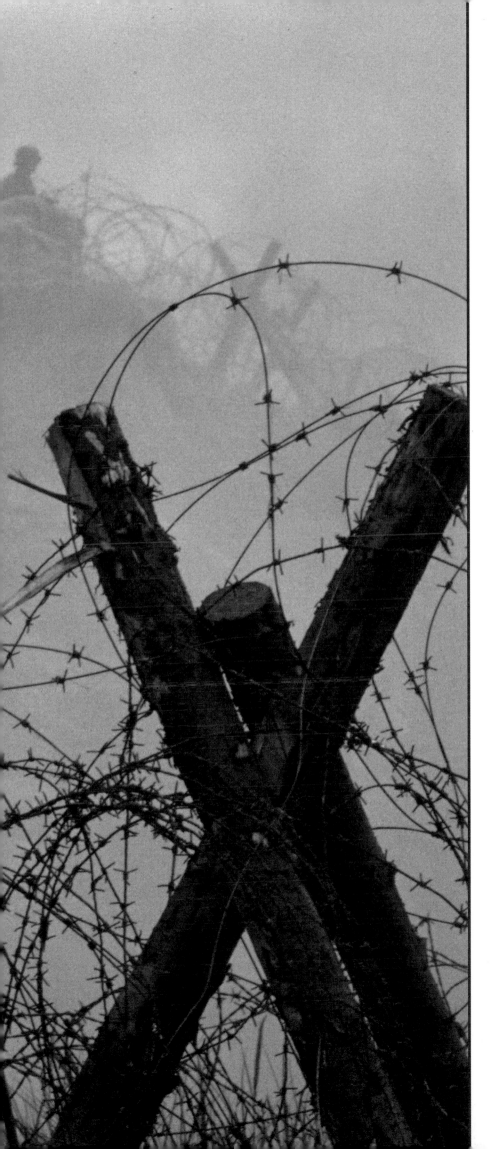

D - D A Y

The U.S. Army's infantry divisions were not elite, by definition, but they had some outstanding characteristics.

The American Selective Service System was just that, selective. One-third of the men called to service were rejected after physical examinations, making the average draftee brighter, healthier, and better educated than the average American. He was twenty-six years old, five feet eight inches tall, weighed 144 pounds, had a thirty-three-and-a-half-inch chest, and a thirty-one-inch waist. After thirteen weeks of basic training, he'd gained seven pounds (and converted many of his original pounds from fat to muscle) and added at least an inch to his chest. Nearly half the draftees were high-school graduates; one in ten had some college. As Geoffrey Perret puts it in his history of the U.S. Army in World War II, "These were the best-educated enlisted men of any army in history."

At the end of 1943 the U.S. Army was the greenest army in the world. Of the nearly fifty infantry, armored, and airborne divisions selected for participation in the campaign in northwest Europe, only two—the 1st Infantry and the 82nd Airborne—had been in combat.

This posed problems and caused apprehension, but it had a certain advantage. According to Pvt. Carl Weast of the U.S. 5th Ranger Battalion, "A veteran infantryman is a terrified infantryman." Sgt. Carwood Lipton of the 506th Parachute Infantry Regiment (PIR) of the 101st Airborne commented, "I took chances on D-Day I would never have taken later in the war. . . ."

For a direct frontal assault on a prepared enemy position, men who have not seen what a bullet or a land mine or an exploding mortar round can do to a human body are preferable to men who have seen the carnage. Men in their late teens or early twenties have a feeling of invulnerability, as seen in the remark of Charles East of the 29th Division. Told by his commanding officer on the eve of D-Day that nine out of ten would become casualties in the ensuing campaign, East looked at the man to his left, then at the man to his right, and thought to himself, "You poor bastards."

—An Excerpt from *D-Day: June 6, 1944*
The Climactic Battle of World War II
by Stephen E. Ambrose

The Men.

June 6, 1944

<u>OFFICE OF THE REGIMENTAL COMMANDER</u>

Soldiers of the Regiment: D-Day

Today, and as you read this, you are en route to that great adventure for which you have trained for over two years.

Tonight is the night of nights.

Tomorrow throughout the whole of our homeland and the Allied world the bells will ring out the tidings that you have arrived, and the invasion for liberation has begun.

The hopes and prayers of your dear ones accompany you, the confidence of your high commanders goes with you. The fears of the Germans are about to become a reality.

Let us strike hard. When the going is tough, let us go harder. Imbued with faith in the rightness of our cause, and the power of our might, let us annihilate the enemy where found.

May God be with each of you fine soldiers. By your actions let us justify His faith in us.

                    Colonel Robert Sink
                    (Memo to his 506th Troopers)

People of Western Europe: A landing was made this morning on the coast of France by troops of the Allied Expeditionary Force...

...I call upon all who love freedom to stand with us now. Together we shall achieve victory.
-- Dwight D. Eisenhower
Broadcast on D-Day

Lt. Den Brotheridge fired a full clip of
thirty-two rounds from his Sten gun. Those
were the first shots fired by the 175,000
British, American, Canadian, Free French,
Polish, Norwegian, and other nationalities in
the Allied Expeditionary Force set to invade
Normandy in the next twenty-four hours.
                    -- Stephen E. Ambrose, D-Day

So the GI hitting the beach in the first wave at Omaha would have
to get through the minefields in the Channel without his LST blowing
up, then get from ship to shore in a Higgins boat taking fire from
inland batteries, then work his way through an obstacle-studded tidal
flat of some 150 meters crisscrossed by machine gun and rifle fire,
with big shells whistling by and mortars exploding all around, to
find his first protection behind the shingle. There he would be
caught in a triple crossfire--machine guns and heavy artillery from
the sides, small arms from the front, mortars coming down from above.

-- Stephen E. Ambrose, D-Day

About seven or eight in the morning, we were being urged by braver and more sensible noncoms and one or two surviving officers to get off the beach and up the bluffs to higher ground. More men from other landing craft behind us were making it across the beach and joining the congestion at the seawall. It would be some time before enough courage returned for us to attempt movement up the slopes and up the beach. Scared, worried, and often praying, I had been busy helping some of the wounded; most of the time, moving in a crouched position, a few of us helped move the helpless to secure areas. Once or twice I was able to control my fear enough to race across the sand to drag a helpless GI from drowning in the incoming tide. That was the extent of my bravery that morning. Then clear thinking replaced some of our fear, and many of us accepted the fact that we had to get off the beach or die where we were. We got off the beach.

-- Harry Parley, Private First Class, Company E, from Voices of D-Day

Normandy was a soldier's battle. It belonged to the riflemen,
machine gunners, mortarmen, tankers, and artillery men who were
on the front lines. There was no room for maneuver. There was no
opportunity for subtlety. There was a simplicity to the fighting:
for the Germans, to hold; for the Americans, to attack.

-- Stephen E. Ambrose, _Citizen Soldiers_

As ranking noncom, I tried to get my men off the boat and make it somehow to the cliff, but it was horrible--men frozen in the sand, unable to move. My radio man had his head blown off three yards from me. The beach was covered with bodies--men with no legs, no arms--God, it was awful. It was absolutely terrible.
   -- Harry Bare, Sergeant, Company F, 1st Squadron, from Voices of D-Day

There was thousands of ships, and we could see landing
boats of American troops. Then came thousands of men at
one time coming on land and running over the beach.
This is the first time I shoot on living men, and
I go to the machine gun and I shoot, I shoot,
I shoot! For each American I see fall,
there came ten hundred other ones!
-- Franz Rachmann, Private,
German 352nd Division,
from Voices of D-Day

.But the hardest lesson to teach in training, the most difficult rule to follow in combat, is to keep moving when fired on. Every instinct makes a soldier want to hug the ground.
                                        -- Stephen E. Ambrose, _Citizen Soldiers_

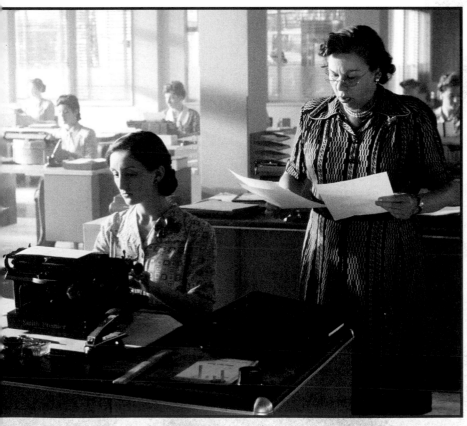

By June 30, the Americans had brought 71,000 vehicles over the beaches (of a planned 110,000) and 452,000 soldiers (of a planned 579,000)...It had eleven divisions in the battle, as scheduled, plus the 82nd and the 101st Airborne... The Americans had evacuated 27,000 casualties. About 11,000 GIs had been killed in action or died of their wounds, 1,000 were missing in action, and 3,400 wounded men had been returned to duty. So the total active duty strength of U.S. First Army in Normandy on June 30 was 413,000. German strength on the American front was somewhat less, while German losses against the combined British-Canadian-American forces were 47,500.

— Stephen E. Ambrose, <u>Citizen Soldiers</u>

The Mission.

29 ON MILLER

Miller and the others look around,
stunned -- we did it. We're alive. After
the beach, it's more than any of them
expected. Nobody says anything, because
there really aren't words to express the
moment. We're here. It's a fact.

Sarge reaches down, picks up a handful of
sand, and pours it into a container that is
already premarked "France." He screws
the tin lid back on and puts it back in his
pack next to two similar tin cans upon
which are crudely inscribed in smeared
blue ink "Africa" and "Italy."

--from the screenplay

Corporal Upham

Sergeant Horvath

Private Jackson

Private Mellish

ON MILLER AND REIBEN

REIBEN
This goes against every-
thing the army taught me.
Makes no sense—

MILLER
What doesn't make sense,
Reiben?

REIBEN
The math, sir. Of this
mission. Maybe you could
explain it to me.

MILLER
What do you want to
know?

REIBEN
Well, sir, in purely
arithmetic terms, what's
the sense in risking eight
guys to save one?

Private Caparzo

Private Reiben

T/4 Medic Wade

Captain Miller

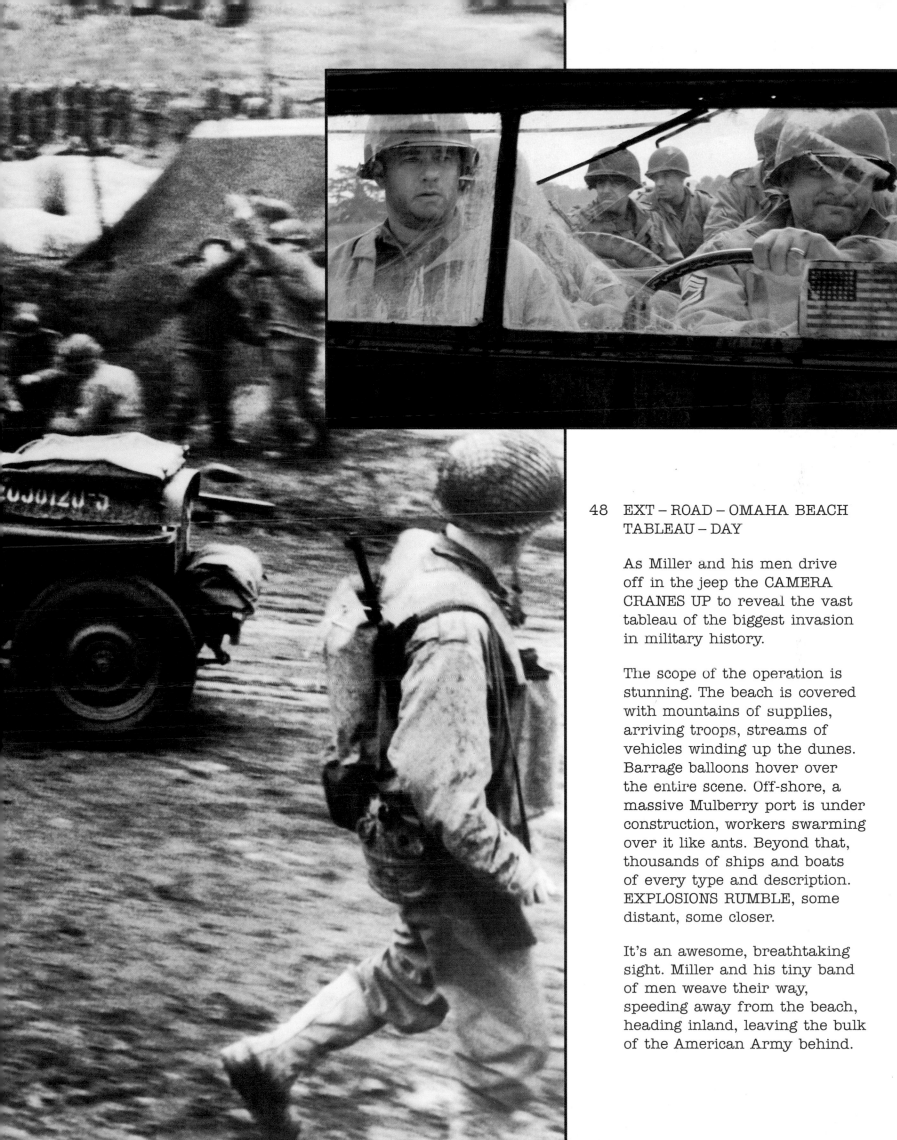

48 EXT – ROAD – OMAHA BEACH
TABLEAU – DAY

As Miller and his men drive
off in the jeep the CAMERA
CRANES UP to reveal the vast
tableau of the biggest invasion
in military history.

The scope of the operation is
stunning. The beach is covered
with mountains of supplies,
arriving troops, streams of
vehicles winding up the dunes.
Barrage balloons hover over
the entire scene. Off-shore, a
massive Mulberry port is under
construction, workers swarming
over it like ants. Beyond that,
thousands of ships and boats
of every type and description.
EXPLOSIONS RUMBLE, some
distant, some closer.

It's an awesome, breathtaking
sight. Miller and his tiny band
of men weave their way,
speeding away from the beach,
heading inland, leaving the bulk
of the American Army behind.

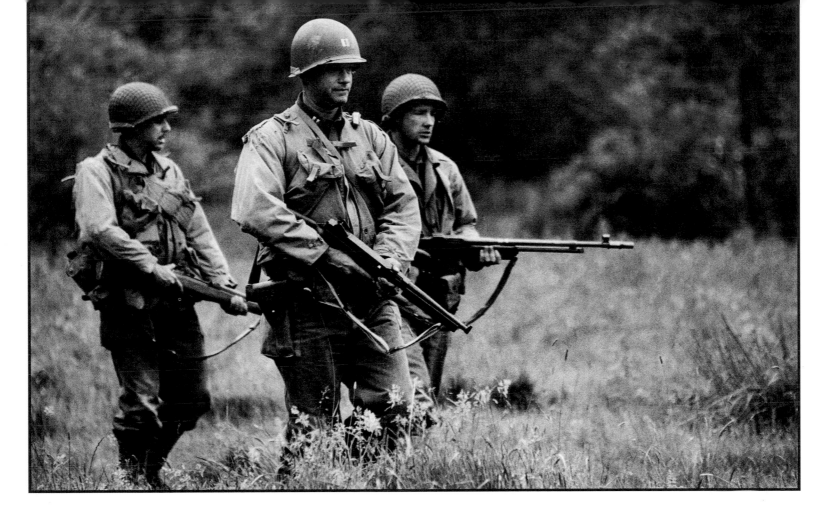

54   EXT.   HEDGEROW CART ROAD – DAY

Miller walks point. His men follow warily. It's hot. They're
exhausted. Upham looks miserable, weighed down like a pack
horse with all the B.A.R. ammunition, slapping at horseflies.
They talk quietly, their eyes scanning.

UPHAM
"War educates the senses, calls into action the will, perfects the
physical constitution, brings men into such swift and close collision
in critical moments that man measures man."

MILLER
I guess that's Emerson's way to look on the bright side.

CAPARZO
Captain. Decent thing to do would be to at least take the kids
down the road to the next town.

MILLER
We're not here to do the decent thing, Caparzo. We're here to
follow orders.

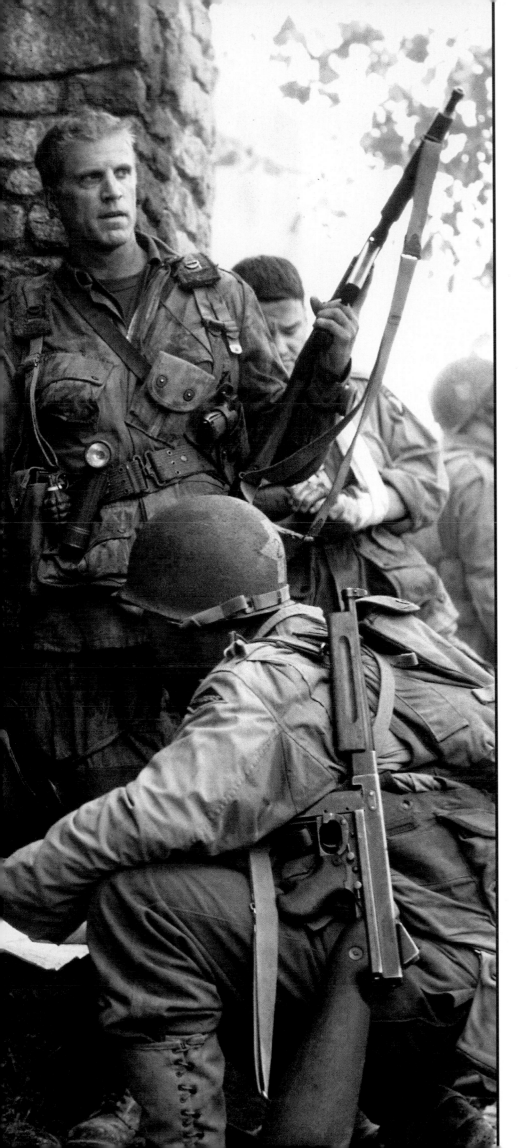

Miller watches his men go. He gives himself
a second and looks at what remains of the
once lovely village, now nothing more than
rubble. Hamill steps up next to him. Though
strangers, Miller and Hamill speak like tired
old friends.

                HAMILL (CONT'D)
        What do you hear? How's it all
        falling together?

                MILLER
        Beachhead's secure but it's slow
        goin'. Monty's takin' his time
        getting to Caen, we can't move
        'til he's ready.

                HAMILL
        That guy's over-rated.

                MILLER
        No kiddin'.

Hamill shakes his head and sighs.

                HAMILL
        We gotta take Caen to take St. Lo.

                MILLER
        And we gotta take St. Lo to take
        Valognes.

                HAMILL
        Gotta take Valognes to take
        Cherbourg.

                MILLER
        Gotta take Cherbourg to take
        Paris.

                HAMILL
        Gotta take Paris to take Berlin.

                MILLER
        Gotta take Berlin to take a boat
        home.

MILLER

Every time you kill one of your men, you
tell yourself you just saved the lives of
two, three, ten, a hundred others. You
know how many men I've lost under
my command?

SARGE

How many?

MILLER
(instantly)

Ninety-four. So that must mean I've
saved the lives of ten times that number.
Maybe twenty, right? See it's simple.
It lets you always choose the mission
over men.

SARGE

Except this time the mission is a man.

Miller looks at Sarge now. His eyes hard.

MILLER

And Ryan better be worth it. He better
go home and cure some disease or invent
a new longer-lasting lightbulb.

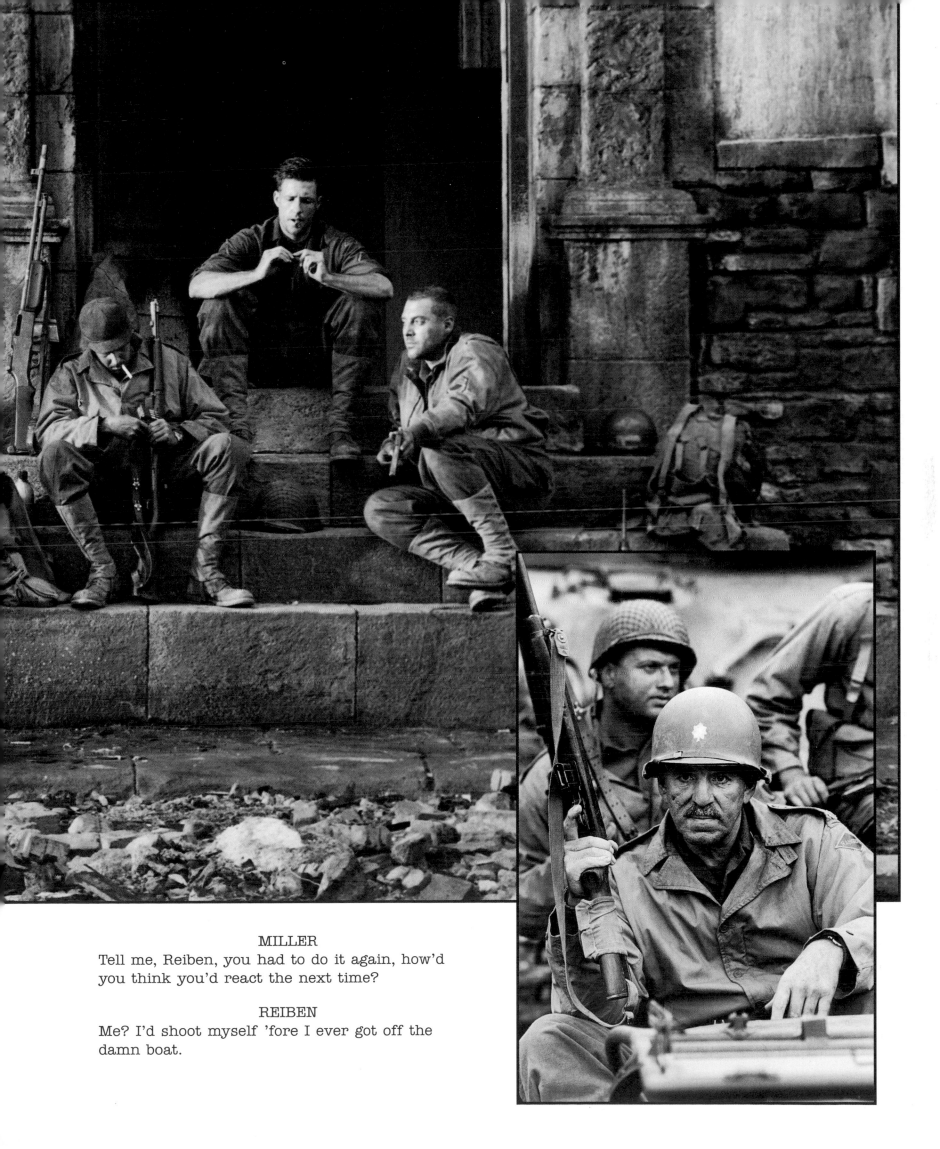

MILLER
Tell me, Reiben, you had to do it again, how'd
you think you'd react the next time?

REIBEN
Me? I'd shoot myself 'fore I ever got off the
damn boat.

Ryan stands, indicates the other guys in his unit.

> RYAN (CONT'D)
> Hell, these guys deserve to go home as much
> as I do. They've fought just as hard.

> MILLER
> Is that what I'm supposed to tell your mother,
> she gets another flag?

> RYAN
> You can tell her that when you found me, I
> was with the only brothers I had left. And that
> there was no way I was deserting them. I think
> she'd understand that.

He and Miller stare at each other.

SARGE

I don't know. Part of me thinks the kid's right,
he asks what he's done to deserve this. He
wants to stay here, fine. Let's leave him and
go home. But then another part of me thinks
what if by some miracle we stay then actually
make it out of here. Someday we might look
back on this and decide that saving Private
Ryan was the one decent thing we were able
to pull out of this whole godawful
mess. Like you said, Capt'n,
maybe we do that, we <u>all</u>
earn the right to go home.

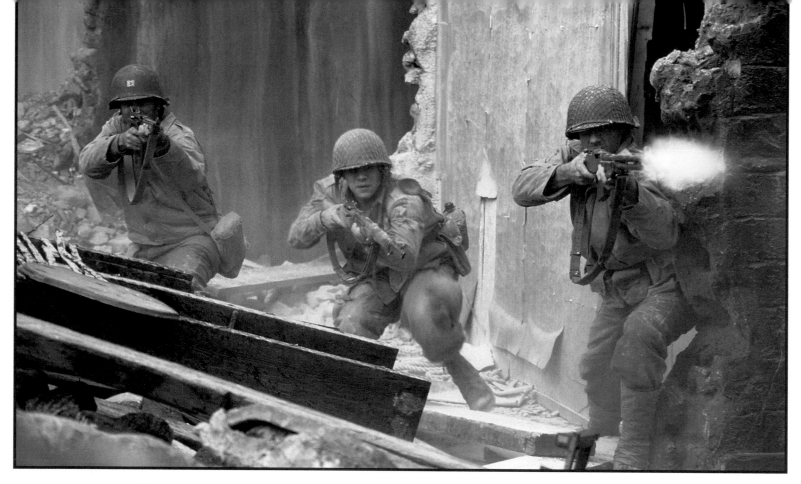

118 ANGLE ON STREET

—and thunderous hell breaks loose as the HAWKINS MINES DETONATE massively along both sides of the street. The walls blow out towards the infantry, taking them down with concussion and shrapnel, killing at least a dozen men...

The MACHINE GUNS OPEN FIRE at the same moment, turning the street into a killing zone

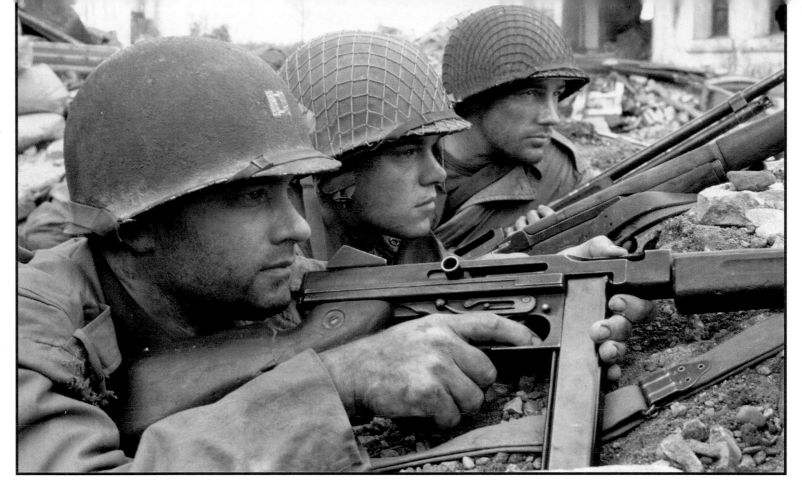

156 THE LAST SANDBAG EMPLACEMENT

... and then the Tiger FIRES ITS CANNON. THE EXPLOSION
TEARS THE WORLD APART, spinning it upside-down, ripping
the air with heat and shrapnel...

... and everything goes quiet, as if the sound has drained out
of the world. We're left with sounds that are remote, faint,
surreal, disembodied...

158 RESUME NORMAL SPEED AND SOUND:

...as a P-51 MUSTANG swoops grandly over the bridge. Tank-buster. It peels overhead, no longer with the sound of voices but with a THROATY ROAR OF A PACKARD ENGINE.

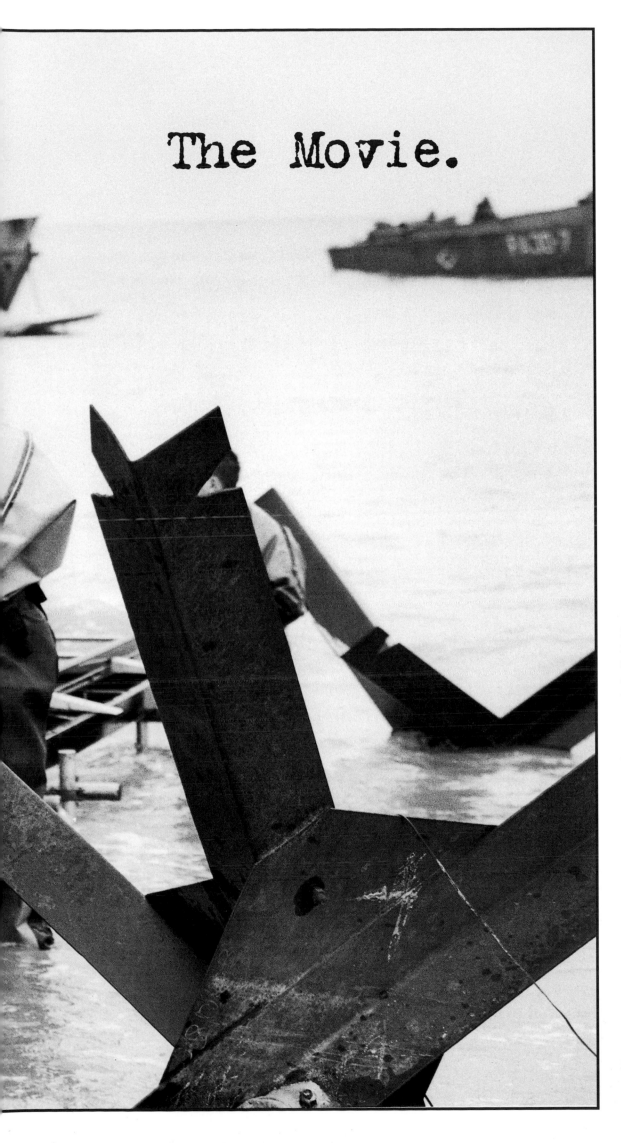

The Movie.

Although I admire war movies and have seen many of them, I wasn't really looking to make a World War II film. I didn't want to shoot the picture as a Hollywood gung-ho Rambo kind of extravaganza. I wanted the audience to be fairly uneasy sitting through the invasion of Normandy.

Our approach to the movie was the way a documentary filmmaker would have approached it in, for example, John Ford's unit shooting the South Pacific War or George Stevens's unit shooting the European campaign. We just had a camera. Janusz stripped all the glossy filters and the filaments from the lenses so they were just like the kind of lenses they actually used in the Second World War. We shot a lot of the war sequences with the shutter speed used by those Bell and Howell cameras of the 1940s for making newsreels.

The audience won't feel much difference except, if we've done our jobs, they will think we were actually on the beach on D-Day.

—Steven Spielberg

"In boot camp, Captain Dye said to us,
'I want you to bring honor to the fraternity
of men who died for your freedom.'"
-- Barry Pepper, actor

The actors in boot camp.
(Left to right) Front row: Barry Pepper,
Tom Hanks, Tom Sizemore, Ed Burns,
Capt. Dale Dye, Vin Diesel,
Adam Goldberg, Giovanni Ribisi,
Jeremy Davies. Back row:
Assistants to Dale Dye.

We went through an extensive training period in the woods for the better part of a week, which helped us understand about the gear and what it's like to slog this stuff around. We're essentially playing guys who are tired and miserable and want to go home. Great physical demands are being made of them constantly.

We hiked all over the place; it was rainy and cold and wet. We slept on the ground and ate food that came out of cans, heated up over little tiny stoves. Dale was constantly yelling at us because we were doing things wrong. We learned various combat techniques but that wasn't as important as the experience itself.

We were up at five in the morning, carrying very heavy stuff on our backs all day long, and we only had a few moments to lie down in the grass and maybe go to sleep. But then we had to get up again; the day's not over until two in the morning.

Now we do that in microcosm as actors, but all of us will tell you that we couldn't have played our parts without experiencing what Dale Dye put us through.

—Tom Hanks

I'm not a wilderness guy. I mean, I'm like the guy in *On the Waterfront* who says, "The crickets make me nervous." I'm a very New York guy. And so already, sleeping out in the wilderness is a stretch for me. And then to sleep under harsh rain conditions and be woken up after only a few hours following a really hard day—it was very rough.

But it did serve two functions. One was the brotherhood. There could not have been a more bonding experience. The other is that our relationship with Tom Hanks couldn't have been set up any better. Every single guy in the platoon wanted to leave early except for Tom who was the only one who said we should stay an extra few days. And it was so appropriate because he's playing the Captain who has the most endurance.

— Vin Diesel, actor

I didn't want to go to boot camp. I'm an actor, I'm going to *act* like a marine, why do I have to *be* a marine? It's called acting, not "being."

We were taken to this forest and given a blanket, no pillow. It was hard to sleep on the ground! In L.A., I don't sleep on the ground, I sleep in a bed.

We got up at four in the morning and ran five miles and did all these push-ups and sit-ups. You don't eat anything and your feet stick out of the tent at night! And since I'm the Sarge, I have to walk around and kick the guys in the feet to wake them up in the morning.

This is nuts, but we really went through something like the men in the movie experienced. In the field, the men would go to their sergeant to voice their grievances and then the sarge went to the captain and that's how it happened in our boot camp. The other actors, Eddie Burns, Vin Diesel, Adam Goldberg, and Jeremy Davies, would come to me to say, "I can't do this."

But then something happened to all of us. We really learned that no one does anything alone in a war. It's all about teamwork—if the other guy's sick or can't get his gear on, you stop and help him out. That's what the marines are all about—it's a brotherhood. We got just a taste of that and it brought us closer together so that when we started shooting we felt a bond.

Still, after boot camp, the first thing I did was drink a Diet Coke.

—Tom Sizemore, actor

Top: **Boot camp.**
Left: (Left to right) Tom Hanks, Capt. Dale Dye, Vin Diesel, Tom Sizemore.

We spent a week together living out in the woods in tents. It was the worst experience of my life. It really was. It was physically exhausting and tough; it was really hard on all of us. But we got a real sense of what these guys went through.

We spent a lot of time talking with Captain Dye, who'd been in Vietnam and Desert Storm. Every night we'd ask him questions about his experiences. What was your relationship with the guys you're serving with? What was it like to lose a friend? And how terrifying was it when you were behind enemy lines and walking around at night in the woods without being able to see five feet in front of you? What's going on in your head?

—Ed Burns, actor

"Steven says, 'Real is the watchword,' and if it looks horrible on screen, well, so it is in combat. The more horrible we can show it, the more people will understand the nobility of the sacrifice that those men made."
—Capt. Dale Dye, USMC (ret.)

The Battle on Omaha Beach scene. (Left to right) Tom Sanders, Production Designer; Steven Spielberg, Director; Tom Hanks, Actor; Capt. Dale Dye, Senior Military Advisor.

I believe there is a certain core spirit within an American fighting man, within a fighting man of any nationality. A certain heart and spirit is common with all fighting men. Actors—who are like dry sponges until you pour on the water—need to be immersed in the rigorous lifestyle, in the horrors facing infantrymen and combat people all over the world. So to the extent that insurance and lifestyles will allow, I immerse those actors in that lifestyle. I take them to the field, I make them eat rations, I shoot at them with blank ammunition, I beat them up, I beat on them, I make them crawl and sleep in the mud and the cold and the dirt. And when they come out the other end, if I've done my job successfully, they have an inkling of what it's like—the deprivations, the hardships people endure to serve their country in the military.
—Capt. Dale Dye, USMC (ret.)

For locations, I looked all around France, Ireland, and England. Ireland had an area that looked exactly like Normandy. The landscape and the beaches were so similar it was uncanny.

We had to have beach access, so we were also looking for a place with a harbor. We needed a particular kind of tide to have a certain amount of beach left when the tide was in, for the crew on the beach.

Also, we needed a location where we could house a thousand-man army and a 45-man crew.

Having worked in Ireland before, we knew we could hire its army, which was a key element. Without a trained army to jump out of the boats and storm the beach with experience, we'd have to train a lot of extras. We needed regiments. We had to get them ready every day and have them on the set.

Logistically, it was a nightmare.

—Tom Sanders, production designer

Crew members on the beach in Ireland.
(Left to right) Steve Painter, Make-up Effects Artist; Mitch Dubin, Camera Operator; Maxie McDonald, Prop Master; Jim Kwiatkowski, Key Grip; Neil Corbould, Special Effects; Janusz Kaminski, Director of Photography; Steven Spielberg, Director; Ian Bryce, Producer; Sergio Mimica, First Assistant Director; Chris Haarhoff, Steadi-Cam/ Camera Operator; Lisa Dean Kavanaugh, Set Decorator.

The tanks and other vehicles were fairly easy to find but not the landing craft. We found some in England and a couple in Scotland, but, interestingly enough, the majority of them were in Palm Springs, California.

We bought them and built cradles to ship them over. They arrived in Southampton and we sent them to a refurbishing yard. Then we put them on another ship and sent them to Ireland. It was a pretty big moving operation for the transportation department.

There are twelve of these landing craft in the movie and several hundred in the background.

—Ian Bryce, producer

One day we were out there on the boats and the Irish sea was really rough. It was a cold, stormy day and the Higgins boats were slamming pretty hard, bouncing and pounding through the surf; the chop was like four to five feet swells. A few of the guys around me were getting sick. We were getting really upset, as in reality, not our characters. We were just very nervous about the water and being in the boats and we got this incredible feeling of impending doom.

It gave me this minute sensation of what it must've been like out there. It was really scary for me. My mind just started to wander and think about how afraid these young guys must have been. And they were so tired and soaking wet. They had all their layers of wool clothing and all their gear and ammunition and when they stepped off the boat, they saw all their pals dying around them. They were so exhausted and seasick and all they could do was crawl up those beaches. And thousands of them lay dead in no time at all. It's unthinkable.

—Barry Pepper, actor

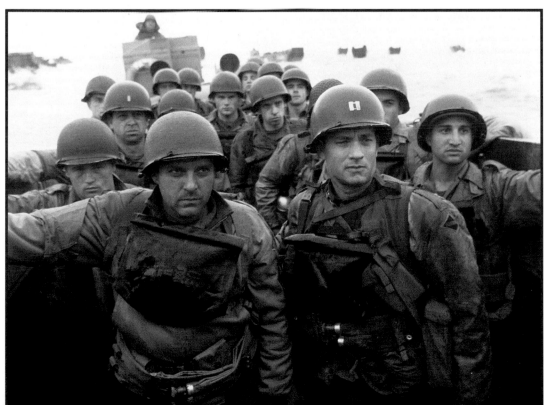

It took us three months to gather the 2,000 weapons that we used in the film. About 500 of them were capable of firing blanks, the others were rubber. They all needed dusting, cleaning, and painting each evening.

We brought them all from England. Some of our weapons came from Germany, but a lot of the American artillery is in England.

Of course, we had to deactivate certain weapons and make sure they weren't capable of firing live ammunition.

—Simon Atherton, armourer

First, I respond emotionally to what the film should look like; the words go through my heart and then I try to put them on the screen.

There were many parallels between this movie and *Schindler's List*. Both were World War II dramas that I envisioned in a semi-documentary style, using hand-held cameras for images that were full of texture. My other idea was to subtract some of the color from the film in a desaturation process done after the movie is shot. About sixty percent of the color was extracted from the final negative.

I didn't want blue skies, I didn't want any clouds. Through the whole course of the movie, there's virtually not a single shot of blue sky. I was going for this kind of burned-out, bleary sky, and I used various techniques to achieve these visuals. For example, Panavision in Los Angeles prepared a particular set of lenses for me. They extracted the protective coating inside the lens so the

images were slightly more defused and prone to flares, and the skies were burned out. The whole image was softer without being out of focus.

Another technique was that we used a different shadow degree to achieve a certain staccato in the actors' movement. We got a crispness of explosions. Everything we shot became slightly, just slightly, more realistic.

—Janusz Kaminski, cinematographer

We're at Hatfield Aerodrome, which is north of London. When we started here, this was a grass field. We decided that it would be better to build a river for environmental reasons and for control. We started from scratch, dug the river back here, and put in the bridge.

We had to build these buildings because we couldn't find anything like this in Europe. It's all historically accurate.

After three trips to France, we built a model of a French village. We made this whole town in model form and then we slowly carved out the places where the bombs would've hit.

The model for this whole town took us five weeks to build in Los Angeles and then we shipped it over here. It's a great tool for the director and the cinematographer to use. They see the set-up in color and in three dimensions.

—Tom Sanders,
production designer

Following page: **Aerial view of the set at Hatfield Aerodrome, which was formerly a grass field.**

Many years ago I was working as a bellman in a hotel, and the guy who picked up the dry cleaning every afternoon and brought it back in the morning was a D-Day veteran. He was away on vacation for two weeks, and when he returned I asked him how it went. He said, "Well, it was both good and it was bad."

He told me that he was a veteran of the 101st Airborne, the paratroopers who jumped on June 5th. Every year he went to this reunion. But every year there were fewer and fewer guys among the group of survivors.

As soon as I read the script for *Saving Private Ryan*, he was one of the first guys who came to my mind.

As a film subject, World War II, by and large, is a never-ending, fascinating lesson for an actor. There was so much about the invasion of Europe that translates in actor's terms: motivations and movement, even the props and costumes.

We started this movie with the utter chaos and shambles of Omaha Beach, which really put everything in its proper perspective. We had lines we never even shot. It was a waste of time to try and establish any kind of rapport amongst us after all the carnage we witnessed.

If we hadn't started with D-Day, and I think Steven would probably agree, we would've wasted an awful lot of time trying to establish other stuff that wasn't important. After D-Day the whole point was: Let's find this guy and get home.

There are a lot of brilliant World War II movies, but it's been thirty years since a real chronicle epic of the war has been made.

For our generation who grew up on various World War II movies, I think that war has a kind of mythical memory connected to being kids and having fathers who were in the war as well as the influence of all those television shows and movies. For the younger generation, it's ancient history. They probably think Normandy is a country right next to Sweden.

Still, we don't want to lecture an audience. We are trying to communicate to them that mere mortals, people who are the same age as themselves, had to be called upon to make this hard sacrifice in service to mankind. From a purely humanistic point of view, I think it's important to go back and examine this piece of history.

—Tom Hanks, actor

Any scene involving the characters as they explore their fragilities are the ones that surprise me the most. I knew that the invasion scenes would work because Steven Spielberg is so accurate about the military and technical aspects. The D-Day landing is very startling, very dramatic, but it's not surprising. But when the actors and the director bring the smaller moments to life, that's when I get startled and I say, "Hey, I didn't write that. Great!"
— Robert Rodat, screenwriter

As a young director observing Spielberg's approach to directing, I've noticed that he's like an undefeated boxer who is so good that he could approach the game without having to plan his shots or his strategy. He can come in, look at the situation, and pick out his shots immediately. He knows how they'll connect and how they'll cut together, so he cuts as he goes along. It's amazing. I've never seen anyone work that fast. Also, he's confident enough with himself to put the priority on the work. If an actor, or anybody else involved in the production, has an idea or a concept, he's completely receptive, which makes all the actors real comfortable.

—Vin Diesel, actor

Left: (Left to right) Tom Hanks,
Steven Spielberg, Ed Burns.
Top: Steven Spielberg, Matt Damon
Right: Jeremy Davies

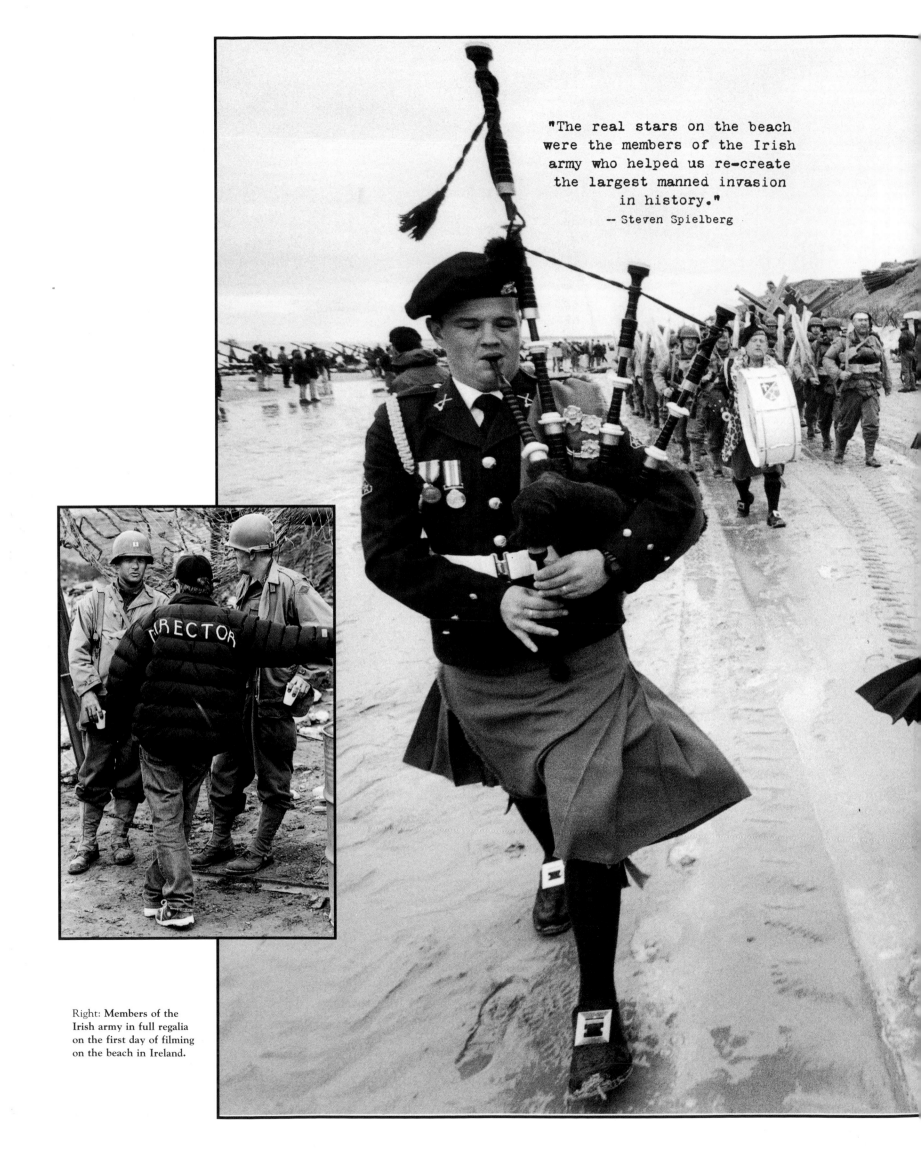

"The real stars on the beach were the members of the Irish army who helped us re-create the largest manned invasion in history."
-- Steven Spielberg

Right: **Members of the Irish army in full regalia on the first day of filming on the beach in Ireland.**

"Omaha Beach was a nightmare. Even now it brings pain to recall what happened there on June 6, 1944. I have returned many times to honor the valiant men who died on that beach. They should never be forgotten. Nor should those who lived to carry the day by the slimmest of margins. Every man who set foot on Omaha Beach that day was a hero."
—General Omar Bradley, 1974

DREAMWORKS PICTURES *and* PARAMOUNT PICTURES
present

An AMBLIN ENTERTAINMENT *Production*

In association with MUTUAL FILM COMPANY

saving private ryan

Directed by STEVEN SPIELBERG

Written by ROBERT RODAT

Produced by STEVEN SPIELBERG & IAN BRYCE

Produced by MARK GORDON & GARY LEVINSOHN

Director of Photography JANUSZ KAMINSKI, A.S.C.

Production Designer TOM SANDERS

Film Editor MICHAEL KAHN, A.C.E.

Music by JOHN WILLIAMS

Costume Designer JOANNA JOHNSTON

Co-Producers BONNIE CURTIS
& ALLISON LYON SEGAN

Casting by DENISE CHAMIAN, C.S.A.

Captain Miller
TOM HANKS

Sergeant Horvath
TOM SIZEMORE

Private Reiben
EDWARD BURNS

Private Jackson
BARRY PEPPER

Private Mellish
ADAM GOLDBERG

Private Caparzo
VIN DIESEL

T/4 Medic Wade
GIOVANNI RIBISI

Corporal Upham
JEREMY DAVIES

Private Ryan
MATT DAMON

Associate Producer/
Production Manager — MARK HUFFAM
First Assistant Director — SERGIO MIMICA-GEZZAN
Second Assistant Director — ADAM GOODMAN
Associate Producer — KEVIN DE LA NOY
Sound Designer — GARY RYDSTROM
Special Effects Supervisor — NEIL CORBOULD
Special Effects Floor Supervisor — CLIVE BEARD
Stunt Coordinator — SIMON CRANE
Supervising Art Director — DANIEL T. DORRANCE
Set Decorator — LISA DEAN KAVANAUGH
Senior Military Advisor — CAPT. DALE DYE, USMC (ret)
U.K. Casting by — PRISCILLA JOHN

THE CAST

Captain Miller — TOM HANKS
Sergeant Horvath — TOM SIZEMORE
Private Reiben — EDWARD BURNS
Private Jackson — BARRY PEPPER
Private Mellish — ADAM GOLDBERG
Private Caparzo — VIN DIESEL
T/4 Medic Wade — GIOVANNI RIBISI
Corporal Upham — JEREMY DAVIES
Private Ryan — MATT DAMON
Captain Hamill — TED DANSON
Sergeant Hill — PAUL GIAMATTI
Lieutenant Colonel Anderson — DENNIS FARINA
Steamboat Willie — JOERG STADLER
Corporal Henderson — MAXIMILIAN MARTINI
Toynbe — DYLAN BRUNO
Weller — DANIEL CERQUEIRA
Parker — DEMETRI GORITSAS
Trask — IAN PORTER
Rice — GARY SEFTON
Garrity — JULIAN SPENCER
Wilson — STEVE GRIFFIN
Lyle — WILLIAM MARSH
Fallon — MARC CASS
Major Hoess — MARKUS NAPIER
Ramelle Paratroopers — NEIL FINNIGHAN
PETER MILES
Field HQ Major — PAUL GARCIA
Field HQ Aide — SEAMUS McQUADE
Coxswain — RONALD LONGRIDGE
Delancey — ADAM SHAW
Lieutenant Briggs — ROLF SAXON
Radioman — COREY JOHNSON
Soldiers on the Beach
LOCLANN AIKEN   JOHN BARNETT
MacLEAN BURKE   VICTOR BURKE
AIDEN CONDRON   PASCHAL FRIEL
SHANE HAGAN   PAUL HICKEY
SHANE JOHNSON   LAIRD MacINTOSH
BRIAN MAYNARD   MARTIN McDOUGALL
MARK PHILLIPS   LEE ROSEN
ANDREW SCOTT   MATTHEW SHARP
VINCENT WALSH   GRAHAME WOOD
Corporal — JOHN SHARIAN
Boyle — GLENN WRAGE
Senior Medical Officer — CROFTON HARDESTER
Czech Wermacht Soldier — MARTIN HUB
Goldman — RAPH TAYLOR
Private Boyd — NIGEL WHITMEY
Private Hastings — SAM ELLIS
German #1 — ERICH REDMAN
German #2 — TILO KEINER
German #3/
Voice on Bullhorn — STEPHAN GROTHGAR
Jean — STEPHAN CORNICARD
Jean's Wife — MICHELLE EVANS
Jean's Son — MARTIN BEATON
Jean's Daughter — ANNA MAGUIRE
Minnesota Ryan — NATHAN FILLION
Lieutenant DeWindt — LELAND ORSER

Paratrooper Lieutenant — MICHAEL MANTAS
Paratrooper Oliver — DAVID VEGH
Paratrooper Michaelson — RYAN HURST
Paratrooper Joe — NICK BROOKS
Paratrooper #1 — SAM SCUDDER
Old French Man — JOHN WALTERS
Old French Woman — DOROTHY GRUMBAR
MP Lieutenant — JAMES INNES-SMITH
General Marshall — HARVE PRESNELL
War Department Colonels — DALE DYE
BRYAN CRANSTON
War Department Captain — DAVID WOHL
War Department Lieutenant — ERIC LOREN
War Department Clerk — VALERIE COLGAN
Mrs. Margaret Ryan — AMANDA BOXER
Ryan as Old Man — HARRISON YOUNG
Old Mrs. Ryan — KATHLEEN BYRON
Ryan's Son — ROB FREEMAN
Ryan's Grandson — THOMAS GIZBERT
Stunts
ANDY BENNETT   JINDRICH KLAUS
PAVEL CAJZL   PAVEL KRATKY
MARC CASS   DEREK LEA
STEVE CASWELL   DIMO LIPITKOVSKI
VIKTOR CERVENKA   GUY LIST
STUART CLARK   DAVID LISTVAN
ARIS COMNINOS   TONY LUCKEN
LAURIE CRANE   SEAN McCABE
RAY DE-HAAN   PETER MILES
JIM DOWDALL   JAN HOLICEK
NEIL FINNIGHAN   RAY NICHOLAS
STEVE GRIFFIN   DONAL O'FARRELL
PAUL HEASMAN   JAROSLAV PETERKA
LYNDON STUART HELLEWELL
GARY POWELL   MARK HENSON
JAROSLAV PSENICKA   PAUL HERBERT
SEON ROGERS   DOMINIC HEWITT
MAC STEINMEIER   JEFF HEWITT-DAVIS
LEOS STRANSKY   JAN HOLICEK
TOM STRUTHERS   MARTIN HUB
PAVEL VOKOUN   DUSAN HYSKA
SHAUN WALLACE   ROB INCH
BILL WESTON   TIDDLER JAMES
MARK HANNA   RAY HANNA

THE CREW

Art Directors — RICKY EYRES
TOM BROWN
CHRIS SEAGERS
ALAN TOMKINS
Standby Art Director — GARY FREEMAN
Assistant Art Director — KEVIN M. KAVANAUGH
Camera Operators — MITCH DUBIN
CHRIS HAARHOFF
SEAMUS CORCORAN
First Assistant Camera — STEVEN MEIZLER
KENNY GROOM
MARK MILSOME
Second Assistant Camera — TOM JORDAN
ROBERT PALMER
Clapper/Loader — ROSALYN ELLIS
Camera Trainees — ALAN HALL
ANGUS MITCHELL
Still Photographer — DAVID JAMES
Sound Mixer — RONALD JUDKINS
Boom Operator — ROBERT JACKSON
Cable Operator — DAVID MOTTA
First Assistant Editors — PATRICK CRANE
RICHARD BYARD
Assistant Editors — MICHAEL TRENT
ALEX GARCIA
SIMON COZENS
BRADLEY SOUBER
Apprentice Editor — JULIE ZUNDER

Supervising Sound Editor — RICHARD HYMNS
Re-Recording Mixers — GARY RYDSTROM
GARY SUMMERS
ANDY NELSON
Video Assist Operator — NOEL DONELLON
Video Assistant — SARAH FRANCIS
Script Supervisor — ANA MARIA QUINTANA
Chief Lighting Technician — DAVID DEVLIN
Rigging Chief Lighting Technician — OSSA MILLS
Best Boys — RICKY PATTENDEN
RICHARD SEAL
Electricians
MAREK BOJSZA   NEIL MONROE
ALAN GROSCH   PETER O'TOOLE
DARREN GROSCH   STEVE PATTENDEN
PAUL KEMP   TERRY TOWNSEND
Key Grips — JAMES KWIATKOWSKI
JOHN FLEMMING
Best Boy Grip — DEREK RUSSELL
Crane Grip — IAN TOWNSEND
"B" Camera Dolly Grip — DAVID RIST
Armourer — SIMON ATHERTON
Assistant Armourers — DEREK ATHERTON
TOMMY DUNNE
KARL SCHMIDT
Property Master — MAXIE McDONALD
Supervising Standby Props — MICKEY PUGH
Standby Props — MICKY WOOLFSON
Chargehand Props — STEPHEN McDONALD
Chargehand Dressing Props — JOHN HOGAN
Property Storage — ROBERT HILL
Props
JOHN FOX   DAVID ROSSITER
BARRY GATES   CHRISTIAN SHORT
CHRISTIAN McDONALD BEN WILKINSON
PHILIP MURPHY
Webbing Supervisor — ANDREW FLETCHER
Webbing Props — STEPHEN BROWN
ALAN HAUSMANN
Production Buyer — DAVID LUSBY
Assistant Set Dressers — VERONIQUE FLETCHER
PHILIPPA McLELLAN
Model Maker — KEITH STEPHEN
Illustrators — MATT CODD
TIM FLATTERY
Art Department
Coordinator — LAVINIA GLYNN-JONES
Art Department Assistants — JOANNA BRANCH
PETER JAMES
ERIC STEWART
Graphic Artist — LAWRENCE O'TOOLE
Draughtsmen — STEPHEN BREAM
WILLIAM HAWKINS
PAUL WESTACOTT
Jr. Draughtsmen — ROBERT COWPER
MARGARET HORSPOOL
Special Effects Workshop
Supervisor — TREVOR WOOD
Lead Sr. Special Effects Technicians
DAVID BRIGHTON   KEVIN HERD
PAUL CORBOULD   DAVE HUNTER
JOHN EVANS
Sr. Special Effects Technicians
JEFF CLIFFORD   MARK MEDDINGS
IAN CORBOULD   MELVYN PEARSON
TERRY COX   PETER PICKERING
KENNETH HERD   PETER WHITE
RAY LOVELL
Special Effects Technicians
MICHAEL BARLETT   JOHN PILGRIM
BRADLEY BARTON   GRAHAM POVEY
DANIEL BENNETT   SIMON QUINN
STEVE BORTHWICK   MELANIE RAYSKI

CAIMIN BOURNE — TONY RICHARDS
CHRISTOPHER BRENNAN — LEE RIDER
ALEX BURDETT — DAVE RODDHAM
PHILIP CLARK — GRANT ROGAN
SIMON COCKREN — KEVIN ROGAN
CLIFF CORBOULD — TIMOTHY STRACEY
MICHAEL CURRAN — PAUL TAYLOR
STUART DIGBY — COLIN UMPELBY
PAUL DIMMER — ANNE MARIE WALTERS
MICHAEL DURKAN — STEVEN WARNER
RAYMOND FERGUSON — DAVID WATKINS
JOHN FONTANA — DAVE WILLIAMS
JOSEPH GEDAY — TREVOR WILLIAMS
ADAM HILLIER — GARETH WINGROVE
ROB MALOS — ALAN YOUNG
DAVE MILLER

Special Effects Buyer — KRISSI WILLIAMSON
Special Effects Coordinator — CAROL McAULAY
Special Effects Assistant Buyer — KATIE GABRIEL
Prosthetics Supervisor — CONOR O'SULLIVAN
Prosthetics Designer — STUART SEWELL
Moldmaking Supervisor — JOHN SCHOONRAAD
Head Sculptor — ANDY HUNT
Prosthetic Crew
  MARTHA FEIN — ROBIN SCHOONRAAD
  EMMA JACKSON — TRISTAN SCHOONRAAD
  BRENDAN LONEGAN — LAURENCE SIMMONS
  DAN NIXON — KATRINA STRACHAN
  JACKIE NOBLE — GAVIN WATTON
Corpse and Animal
Effects Designers — NEILL GORTON / STEVE PAINTER
Corpse and Animal Effects
Coordinator — LINDY DIAMOND
Senior Sculptors
  STUART BRAY — DUNCAN JARMAN
  PAUL CATLING — WALDO MASON
  STUART CONRAN — PHILIP MATHEWS
  ANDY GARNER — COLIN WARE
Technicians
  CATH BLACKETT — WILL PETTY
  CHRIS BYRNE — ANDREW PROCTOR
  ARON COLLINS — LIZ RAGLAND
  LEE CRAIK — GRAHAM ROSS
  ANDREW FRANCE — PATRICK RUSHMERE
  JOANNE FRYE — JANINE SCHNEIDER
  BARRIE GOWER — ROBERT SIMPSON
  NINA GRAHAM — ROSIE SHANNON
  SAM IVES — ANNABEL TAIT
  VERONIQUE KEYS — BILL TURPIN
  ROB MAYOR — TANIA WANSTALL
  NICOLA O'TOOLE — SIMON WEBBER
  SUZI OWEN — JAMES WESTON
  ANTHONY PARKER — SHELLI WOODALL
Costume Supervisor — PAM WISE
Assistant Costume Designer — SALLY TURNER
Military Costumer — DAVID CROSSMAN
Costume Department Key — PATRICK WHEATLEY
Wardrobe Master — ANTHONY BLACK
Crowd Wardrobe Master — DAVE WHITEING
Key Set Costumer — TOM McDONALD
Set Costumers — MARCUS LOVE-McGUIRK / ADAM ROACH / LAURA MAY
Costumers — NIGEL BOYD / RUPERT STEGGLE / PETER EDMONDS
Key Costume Breakdown — TIMOTHY SHANAHAN
Costume Breakdown — THOMAS LIGHTFOOT / EMMA WALKER / NICOLA RAPLEY
Key Costume Special Effects/
Stunts — PHILIP GOLDSWORTHY

Costume Special Effects/
Stunts — PETER HORNBUCKLE
Workroom Head — DAVID EVANS
Seamstress — PAT WILLIAMSON
L.A. Key Costumer — DIANA WILSON
Costume Coordinator — SARAH HINCH
Costume Production Assistants — NATALIE ROGERS / HELEN JEROME
Key Makeup Artist — LOIS BURWELL
Key Second Makeup Artist — PAULINE HEYS
Mr. Hanks' Makeup Artist — DANIEL C. STRIEPEKE
Makeup Artists — SIAN GRIGG / CATHERINE HEYS
Trainee Makeup — POLLY EARNSHAW
Chief Hairstylist — JEANETTE FREEMAN
Hairstylist — TAPIO SALMI
Production Controller — JIM TURNER
Supervising Production Accountant — CAROLYN HALL
Production Accountant — GEORGE MARSHALL
Financial Representative — JAMES T. LINVILLE
Assistant Production Accountants — SOPHIE DASIC / LISA-KIM LING KUAN
Accounting Assistants — CLAIRE KENNY / ANDREW PYKE / FRY MARTIN
Post Production Accountant — MARIA DeVANE
Production Coordinator — LIL HEYMAN
Assistant Production Coordinators — TANIA CLARKE / LULU MORGAN / RICK A. OSAKO
Second Second
Assistant Director — KAREN RICHARDS
Third Assistant Directors — MARTIN KRAUKA / ANDREW WARD
Unit Publicist — SUE D'ARCY
Location Managers — ALEX GLADSTONE / ROBIN HIGGS
Assistant Location Managers — SIMON BURGESS / KATRYNA SAMUT-TAGLIAFERRO / REBECCA JONES / HUGO SMITH-BINGHAM
Assistants to Mr. Spielberg — KERI WILSON / MARC FUSCO
Assistants to Mr. Spielberg – L.A. — SUSAN RAY / ELIZABETH NYE
Assistant to Mr. Bryce — CARLYLE FAIRFAX SMITH
Assistant to Ms. Curtis — MARK RUSSELL
Assistant to Mr. Hanks — SHARON AIKEN
Production Associate — JASON ROBERTS
Production Assistants
  JANE BURGESS — GAIL MUNNELLY
  CARLOS FIDEL — AINE STACEY
Military Advisor — JOHN BARNETT
Casting Assistant – U.K. — ORLA PULTON
Casting Assistants – L.A. — KARA J. KATSULIS / JEFF McNALLY
Construction Coordinator — TERRY APSEY
Assistant Construction Coordinator — JOHN NEW
Construction Buyer — HILLERY COPE
Supervising Carpenters — JOHN McGREGOR / PAUL WILLIAMSON / ANTHONY YOUD
Chargehand Carpenters — ALAN BOOTH / FRED MYATT / PHILLIP SMITH
Wood Machinists — NORMAN BAKER / WILLIAM SOWER
Storesman — LOUIS KING
H.O.D. Plasterer — ALLAN CROUCHER
Supervising Plasterers — PETER BLACK / MALCOLM MISTER
Chargehand Plasterer — KEITH SHANNON
Chargehand Plasterer Labourer — DAVID SILVERTON

H.O.D. Painter — ADRIAN START
Supervisor Painter — BRIAN MORRIS
H.O.D. Stagehand — KENNETH STACHINI
Chargehand/Stagehand — NIGEL ROSS
H.O.D. Rigger — RON NEWVELL
Supervisor Rigger — STEVEN POLLECUTT
Chargehand Rigger — JOHN NEWVELL
Welder — CHRISTOPHER ROSE
Welder Fabricator — COLIN GIBBS
Assistant Welder — MARK McBARRON
Plant Engineers — PAUL MALING / STEVE TAYLOR
Standby Rigger — GINGER MacARTHY
Standby Carpenter — MICKY LAW
Standby Painter — JOE MONKS
Standby Plasterer — DEREK SMITH
Standby Stagehand — GERRY DELANEY
Transportation Coordinator — BRIAN HATHAWAY
Transportation Captain — BRIAN BAVERSTOCK
Mr. Spielberg's Driver — JOHN COLEMAN
Mr. Hanks' Driver — DAVID ROSENBAUM
Mr. Bryce's Driver — MIKE FAULKNER
Unit Drivers
  GARY BIRMINGHAM — BRUCE NEIGHBOUR
  FREDDIE CHIVERTON — SEAN O'CONNOR
  KEITH HORSLEY — BILLY TURNER
  BARRY LEONTI
Picture Vehicles by — PLUS FILM SERVICES
Picture Vehicle Coordinator — STEVE LAMONBY
Mechanics
  DAVE FORSTER — MICHAEL TOMBS
  ANDY GRAY — PETER TOMBS
  JOHN LEHEN — JOHN SYMONDSEN
Catering Services Provided by — SET MEALS
Catering Manager — DAVID REYNOLDS
Manager — SARA CHAPPELL
Head Chefs — COLIN ANDERSON / SINJUN SMITH
Chef — ED ANDERSON
Assistant Chefs — SARAH LINTON / BECKY WISEMAN
Nurse — CARRIE JOHNSON
Fire Safety Officer — DAVID DEANE
Firemen — CHRISTOPHER CULLUM / BOB POLLARD

IRISH UNIT

Production Manager — SEAMUS McINERNEY
Camera Operator — CIAN DE BUTLEAR
First Assistant Camera — CIARAN BARRY / DONAL GILLIGAN
Second Assistant Camera — DECLAN KING / DOCHY J. LOWE
Chief Lighting Technician — TERRY MULLIGAN
Grip — PHILIP MURPHY
Electricians — GARRET BALDWIN / PETER O'TOOLE
Props — WILLIAM DRAPER / GARY WIFFEN / COS EGAN
Senior Special Effects
Technician — GERRY JOHNSTON
Special Effects Technicians — MICHAEL KEARNS / KEVIN NOLAN / ANDREW NOLAN
Marine Coordinator — ROBIN DAVIES
Marine Safety — ALISTER RUMBALL
Marine Riggers — DAN BRITTON / ROGER McGOWAN
Shipwright — PAUL TINGEY
Marine Engineers — DAVE LESHONE / GEOFF RALEIGH
Landing Craft Coordinator — KEN MURGATROYD

Landing Craft Crew
ALAN ARMSBY   JOHN MURPHY
RUPERT BARNES   NOEL MURPHY
COLIN BATES   DAVID NEED
ROBERT BRIAN   MICHAEL O'LEARY
STEPHEN DAWSON   STEVE RICHARDS
PATRICK DEVEREUX   GARY ROWE
ROBERT FOLEY   MICK SELLEN
DONALD HIND   STEVE SWEET
JOHN GEAR   MICK THOMAS
DAVID KELLY   RAY TOVEY
JAMES KINSELLA   GERALD WADE
RONNIE LONGRIDGE   BRIAN WALKER
DAVID McDOWALL   SEAMUS WALSH
JASON MOONEY   STUART WESTON
LINDSAY MOORE   DAVID WINN
PETER MOORE
Costume Supervisor   SHEILA FAHEY
Costume Assistants
FIONA BELTON   OONA McFARLAND
MAEVE HUNTER   ANN O'HALLORAN
COLETTE JACKSON   ANN REGAN
LOUISE KEATING
Makeup Artists   JENNIFER HEGARTY
                            AILBHE LE MASS
Hairstylist   MARTINA McCARTHY
Assistant Hairstylist   HUGH McALLISTER
Second Assistant Director   CATHERINE DUNNE
Third Assistant Directors   DAISY CUMMINS
                            BARBARA MULCAHY
                            HANNAH QUINN
Location Manager   MELANIE GORE GRIMES
Assistant Location Managers JAMES CLONEY
                            DAVID MORRIS
Production Accountant   DAVID MURPHY
Assistant Production
    Accountants   ANN-MARIE FITZGERALD
                            SIOBHAN SWEENEY
Production Coordinator   ELAINE BURT
Asst. Production Coordinator CLODAGH BOWERS
Sign Writer   LAURENCE O'TOOLE
Construction Managers   MICHAEL DEEGAN
                            DAVID LOWERY
Production Office Assistants
MAEVE BUTLER   DICKON LEVINGE
AILEEN CURTIN   KATHLEEN LUCKING
LISA DRAYNE
Nurse   SIOBHAN GRANT
Post Production Executive   MARTIN COHEN
Post Production Supervisor ERICA FRAUMAN
Post Production Coordinator SVEN E. FAHLGREN
Post Production Sound
Services Provided by   SKYWALKER SOUND
    a division of Lucas Digital Limited, Marin County, CA
Effects Editors
ETHAN VAN DER RYN   TERESA ECKTON
FRANK EULNER   KAREN WILSON
LARRY OATFIELD
Dialogue Editors   GWENDOLYN YATES WHITTLE
                            SARA BOLDER
                    EWA SZTOMPKE OATFIELD
Foley Editors   SANDINA BAILO LAPE
                            BRUCE LACEY
Assistant Sound Designer   SHANNON MILLS
Supervising Sound Assistants LISA CHINO
                            ANDRÉ FENLEY
Assistant Effects Editors   DAN ENGSTROM
                            LARRY HOKI
Assistant Dialogue Editor   MARY WORKS
Assistant Foley Editor   SUSAN POPOVIC
Sound Intern   GERARD ROCHE
Machine Room Supervisor   RONALD G. ROUMAS
Mix Technician   TONY SERENO

Machine Room Operator   CHRISTOPHER BARRICK
Sound Transfer Supervisor   MARNI L. HAMMETT
Digital Transfer   JONATHAN GREBER
                            DEE SELBY
Video Services   CHRISTIAN VON BURKLEO
                            JOHN TORRIJOS
ADR Supervisor   LARRY SINGER
ADR Editors   DENISE WHITING
                            THOMAS WHITING
ADR Assistant   STEPHANIE D. KRIVACEK
ADR Mixer   DEAN DRABIN
ADR Recordist   CARY STRATTON
Foley Artists   DENNIE THORPE
                            JANA VANCE
Foley Mixer   TONY ECKERT
Foley Recordist   FRANK MEREL
Re-Recordists   RUDI PI
                            MATT COLLERAN
Engineer   TOM LALLEY
ADR Group Coordinator   MICKIE McGOWAN
Additional Re-Recording Services   TODD-AO
                            STUDIOS WEST
Music Editor   KEN WANNBERG
Assistant Music Editor KELLY MAHAN JARAMILLO
Post Production Associate   MIKE CUEVAS
Orchestrations   JOHN NEUFELD
    Score performed by members of the Boston Symphony
    Orchestra and by the Tanglewood Festival Chorus
Orchestral Personnel Manager   LYNN G. LARSEN
Horn Solos   GUS SEBRING
Trumpet Solos   TIM MORRISON   THOMAS ROLFS
Recorded and Mixed by   SHAWN MURPHY
Score Recorded at   SYMPHONY HALL, BOSTON
Scoring Consultant   SANDY DeCRESCENT
Music Preparation   JO ANN KANE MUSIC SERVICE
Executive in Charge of Music   TODD HOMME
Special Visual
Effects by   INDUSTRIAL LIGHT & MAGIC
    A division of Lucas Digital Limited, Marin County, CA
Visual Effects Supervisor   STEFEN FANGMEIER
Visual Effects Co-Supervisor   ROGER GUYETT
Visual Effects Producer   KIM BROMLEY
Associate Visual Effects Producer   HEATHER SMITH
Visual Effects Art Director   ALEXANDER LAURANT
Color Timing Supervisor   KENNETH SMITH
CG Sequence Supervisor   GREGOR LAKNER
Sabre Supervisor   PABLO HELMAN
CG Artists
KATHLEEN BEELER   TERRY CHOSTNER
GONZALO ESCUDERO   BRIDGET GOODMAN
JOANNE HAFNER   MARY McCULLOCH
JENNIFER McKNEW   CHRISTA STARR
PAUL THEREN
Sabre Artists   CAITLIN CONTENT
                            CHAD TAYLOR
Digital Matte Artist   MATTHEW HENDERSHOT
Visual Effects Production Coordinator   LORI ARNOLD
Visual Effects Editor   BILL KIMBERLIN
Scanning Supervisor   JOSHUA PINES
Visual Effects Camera
Operator   MARTIN ROSENBERG
Visual Effects Camera Assistant   ROBERT HILL
Lead Effects Technician   GEOFF HERON
Effects Technician   DAN NELSON
Stage Technicians   CARL ASSMUS
                            BERNY DEMOLSKI
                            ROBERT DOHERTY
Film Scanning Operator   GEORGE GAMBETTA
Negative Line-up   TIM GEIDEMAN
Plate Restoration   TRANG BACH
Digital Production
KATHLEEN DAVIDSON   JENNIFER GONZALEZ
GARRICK MEEKER   ERIN WEST

Digital Technologies   DANNY LEE
                            JEFFREY YOST
Visual Effects Production
Assistant   AMANDA MONTGOMERY
Color Timer   DALE GRAHN
Negative Cutter   GARY BURRITT
Titles & Opticals   PACIFIC TITLE/MIRAGE

SONGS
"Solitude" Written by Duke Ellington, Irving Mills &
                            Eddie DeLange

"Tu Es Partout"   Written by Edith Piaf &
                            Marguerite Monnot
"C'était Une Histoire
D'Amour"   Written by Henri Contet & Jean Jal
                            Performed by Edith Piaf
                        Courtesy of Mercury Records, France
            By arrangement with PolyGram Film & TV Music

Soundtrack Available on
DREAMWORKS RECORDS

Produced with the support of investment incentives
for the Irish film industry provided by the
government of Ireland.

THE PRODUCERS WISH TO THANK
THE FOLLOWING:
The British Film Commission
Welwyn Hatfield District Council
St. Albans District Council
The Residents of Welwyn & Hatfield
Herts Film Link
Arlington Property Developments
Irish Department of Arts, Culture and the Gaeltacht
Irish Department of Defense and Defense Forces
Irish Department of the Marine
The Cloney Family
Wexford County Council
The Residents of the City and
County of Wexford, Ireland
St. Peters College, Wexford
The U.S. Department of Defense
The American Battle Monuments Commission
20-20 Extras Casting
Fruit of the Loom
Range Rover
Mar-Key Marquees
Lee Lighting

Filmed on location in England, Ireland and France

Edited on the Moviola™

ACKNOWLEDGEMENTS
The publisher and editors wish to thank the
following for their special contributions to this book:
Stephen E. Ambrose, Sharon Black, Sheila Clarke,
Bonnie Curtis, Laura Fox, Brad Globe, Tom Hanks,
David James, Suzanne Jurva, Jane LeGate, Marvin Levy,
Anne McGrath, Randy Nellis, Boyd Peterson,
Terry Press, Robert Rodat, Mark Russell,
Heidi Schaeffer, Jerry Schmitz, Steven Spielberg,
Michael Vollman, Hurley West,
and Stephanie Wheeler.